My Part of the Story

Exploring Identity in the United States

FACING
HISTORY &
OURSELVES

Facing History & Ourselves uses lessons of history to challenge teachers and their students to stand up to racism, antisemitism, and other forms of bigotry and hate. For more information about Facing History & Ourselves, please visit our website at www.facinghistory.org.

Copyright © 2017 by Facing History & Ourselves, Inc. All rights reserved.

Facing History & Ourselves® is a trademark registered in the US Patent & Trademark Office.

Cover art credit: AdobeStock

Last updated June 2025.

ISBN: 978-1-940457-22-2

My Part of the Story was developed in collaboration with Boston Public Schools. We are grateful for the teachers who piloted the lessons and provided important feedback that helped to shape and improve this unit.

Contents

Unit Overview

Essential Question

- **What is the identity of the United States, and how do I fit into it?**

Introduction

This unit is a collection of six lessons designed to launch a course about United States history, literature, or civic life through an examination of students' individual identities. Adolescence is a time when many young people struggle with issues of independence, trust, freedom, and responsibility. It is also a time when life centers around peer groups and mutual relationships. The materials in this unit support and challenge students in their efforts to define their own identity and their relationship to society as a whole. This approach empowers students to develop their own voices in both the classroom and the world at large, and it engages students in a study of the United States by showing them that their voices are integral to the story of the country.

Students will begin the unit by reflecting on their own choices and circumstances to better understand themselves and their experiences. Next, they will examine the factors that help make each of us who we are, including the influences of names, labels, choices, and family legacies, and from there students will begin to examine what makes up the identity of the United States, exploring how individuals and groups have defined what makes the nation what it is. The final lessons and activities in the unit help students both to understand that the identity of the United States is dynamic, not static, and to see that their choices and their stories fuel this dynamism.

Throughout the unit, students will read and discuss texts, as well as watch videos and create visual representations of identity. All of the activities are meant to develop their understanding of how we all become who we are and how we all contribute, in different ways, to our national context. For students living in the United States, the unit is meant to help them see how their personal stories are part of the greater national narrative. For those living outside the United States, the lessons will help them explore their own identities, and hopefully the same learning about personal and national identity will transfer to their own context.

The impact of this unit will be heightened if the course that follows is designed to revisit regularly the complexity of both individual and national identity. The strategies used here to help students explore the factors that influence their own identities can be adapted to analyze and build historical empathy for individuals in history and deeper understanding of characters in literature. The engagement that this unit ignites in students can be sustained throughout the entire year if the course is constructed to be inclusive of the experiences and perspectives of the diversity of individuals and groups who have made crucial contributions to the history, literature, and culture of the United States.

Learning Goals

Students will understand that:

- Identity is dynamic, complex, and personal, and it affects both how we see ourselves and how we interact with others.
- Our environment influences how we understand ourselves and others.
- The identity of a nation like the United States is the product of collaboration and conflict between a variety of individual voices and groups—some famous, but many not.

Students will be able to:

- Cite specific textual evidence to support analysis of primary and secondary sources.
- Compare and contrast treatments of the same topic in several primary and secondary sources.
- Make connections between the history and literature they study and their current lived experience.

Finding Your Voice

Materials

IMAGE:
Flag of Faces

READING:
Coming to America,
Finding Your Voice

Find the materials you will need
to teach this lesson plan at
hstry.is/mypart.

Essential Question

- **How does each person's story contribute to the larger narrative of United States history?**

Overview

The goal of this first lesson is to help students consider why, before they embark on their study of United States history, literature, or civics, it is helpful to first consider their individual identities. Students will begin by defining what it means to them, as they begin this unit, to be American. (This is a definition that they will return to and refine throughout the unit.) Then they will begin to consider the idea that the identity and history of the United States is the product of a multitude of individual perspectives, voices, and choices. By understanding their own identities and the stories about how they and their families arrived at this moment in this place, they can begin to understand how they both contribute to and are affected by the larger history of the country. Finally, students will consider the power of their voices and the effect their personal stories can have not only on their friends, families, and communities but also the identity and history of the United States.

Activities

1. Activate Our Own Assumptions

In this opening activity, students will begin the unit by reflecting on what "American" means to them. Their ideas about this topic may change throughout the unit, as well as over the span of the history or literature course they are beginning.

- Ask students to take out a blank piece of paper and draw a picture of what they think an "American" looks like.

- After a few minutes, have them share and discuss their pictures with a partner, asking the following questions: How did you each decide what to draw? How are the pictures similar? How are they different?

- Discuss together: Where might our ideas of what it means to be "American" come from? Where do we hear messages about what "American-ness" can be?

2. Analyze the "Flag of Faces"

This brief activity invites students to analyze an image of an American flag comprised of a variety of individual faces. The flag serves as a useful metaphor for the relationship between individuals and the national identity of the United States.

- Display the image of the Flag of Faces from the Ellis Island Immigration Museum.

- Give students a minute to look quietly at the image. Instruct them to record in their journals three things they notice about the image.

- Then lead them in a class discussion of the image based on these prompts:

  - What flag is represented in this image?

  - What faces are represented? What do you notice about the variety of faces?

  - What do flags typically symbolize? Where do they appear? How do people often respond to them?

  - What do you think this representation of a flag is meant to symbolize? How is its meaning similar to or different from what you drew in the previous activity?

  - This image is part of an interactive digital exhibit in the museum on historic Ellis Island (where millions of immigrants entered the United States). Why might someone have decided to create an exhibit about the United States that is constantly changing and being updated?

- If it does not emerge from the discussion, explain to students that, just as these faces of individuals contribute to the whole image of the flag, individual identities and stories contribute to the identity of a group or country and its historical narrative. The history and culture of the United States, for example, has always been shaped by the interaction of individuals—some famous, many not—from a variety of backgrounds and origins. Explain to students that they will begin the year with an examination of their own identities and stories so that they can better understand their roles in the larger national story.

3. Read and Discuss the "Coming to America" Story

Students will read Coming to America, Finding Your Voice. In this text, journalist Maria Hinojosa describes how she learned from her mother to find and use her voice, even when she feels powerless. Hinojosa begins the reading by noting that having a "coming to America" story is a universal experience, even for non-immigrants, since everyone has a story about how they arrived in their present life and circumstances.

- As a whole class, read Coming to America, Finding Your Voice. Students should read the piece twice together, first for comprehension and then to consider ideas and themes to guide their thinking.

- After the first reading, have students reflect on and discuss the following comprehension questions in pairs or triads, and then debrief their answers as a whole group:
  - What does *here* mean at the end of the first paragraph, and why do you think it is in quotation marks?
  - Why does Hinojosa put quotation marks around the phrase "real America"? What is she implying about that idea?
  - What details does Hinojosa include to describe the differences between her mother and the immigration agent? How do those details support the statement, "My mom didn't feel very powerful"?
  - How did Hinojosa's mother make the big Texan feel small?
  - What lesson does Hinojosa say she learned from her mother in her "coming to America" story?
- After the second reading, lead a class discussion using the following analysis questions:
  - What is Hinojosa saying about the value of each person's story?
  - What message is Hinojosa trying to deliver to young people who might feel alone or different?
  - How might you connect Hinojosa's story to the Flag of Faces? Does it connect to the image you drew in the first activity?
  - Hinojosa starts her essay by saying that we all have a "coming to America" story. However, it is important to acknowledge that some groups chose to come to this country, while others were forced. This unit is called My Part of the Story, and it's important to give students space to share their part, even if it is not represented in the resources in this unit. For this reason, we recommend asking a question such as: How is Hinojosa's experience of the United States similar to your own? How is it different?
- At the end of class or for homework, ask students to respond to *one* of the following prompts in their journals:
  - Describe a time when you felt voiceless or powerless. What led you to feel that way?
  - Describe a time when your voice was strong. What helped you to find the "power in your gut"?

AP Photo / Jon Elswick

The "Flag of Faces" exhibit at the Ellis Island Immigration Museum is a mosaic of individual portraits.

Flag of Faces

Coming to America, Finding Your Voice

In 2010, journalist Maria Hinojosa shared her "coming to America" story in the foreword to a book of writing by Boston high school students:

We all have a "coming to America" story. Whether you were brought to this country as a baby immigrant like me or whether you were born in South Boston, we all have a story of how we got to this "here."

When I was almost two years old, my mom traveled from Mexico by plane with me and my two older brothers and sister. We were on our way to meet my dad, who had already moved to Chicago. We would live there first and then make our way to Brookline. But on this day, we had to pass the immigration checkpoint at the Dallas airport before we made our connection to Chicago.

The super-tall Texan immigration agent with the super-thick accent towered over my five-foot-tall mom who also had a very thick accent—a Mexican one. The agent inspected all of our green cards, looked my mom and the four kids up and down and apparently sideways, and then he bellowed out an order: "You are welcome to come into this country . . . " he said, his drawl lingering. But then he looked at me. "Everyone but that little baby. I can see a rash on her skin and she will have to stay in quarantine."

My mom didn't feel very powerful as she was being looked down upon and ordered to leave her baby behind in a new country. But she reached deep down inside and found her power in her gut and puffed up all the five feetness of her tiny body as tall as she could. And then, as if a volcano erupted inside her, she found her voice. She *trusted* her voice. And she looked up at that agent and said, "No sir! I weel not leeve my daughter here with chu. She is coming with me. She eez not sick! And I weel not leeve without her. Do you HEAR ME? I weel not leeve her here!"

The tall Texan suddenly felt very small next to my mother's big and powerful voice. "Yes, ma'am," he said. "You can all come in. I am sorry!"

Ever since I heard my coming to America story, I have used it as an inspiration to find my own gut, my own power, my own voice when I feel powerless. If mom could do that almost 50 years ago—tiny and accented and in a new country—I can surely find my own voice when I feel tiny and unheard and powerless.

Sometimes when you feel invisible, it's easy to feel voiceless. And when you feel voiceless, then you learn how to not use your voice. And when you don't use your voice, you don't hear yourself. And when you don't hear yourself, it's hard to trust who you are.

But with my coming to America story, my mom showed me that words are power. Your voice is your instrument—whether you speak (with an accent or not), write, sing or shout. It can be a literal sound or it can be your voice on a piece of paper or a computer screen. But it is yours. And it comes from *your* gut. So maybe you should trust it.

I remember thinking because I was a bit different, no one else saw the world like I did. I was a Mexican immigrant kid growing up on the south side of Chicago. There weren't a lot of other kids like me. I did feel different. I felt small. At times I felt voiceless. I thought I was the only student who felt powerless and not part of the "real America." I know now that wasn't the case. I know now that many kids felt different but we just didn't talk about this. Ever.[1]

1 Maria Hinojosa, foreword to *We Turned Back to See Where We Came From: Snapshots, Vignettes, and Stories* (Boston, MA: 826 Boston, 2010).

LESSON
Identity and Names

Materials

📖 **READING:**
Choosing Names

📖 **READING:**
Two Names, Two Worlds

📄 **HANDOUT:**
Online-Search Identity Chart

✏️ **TEACHING STRATEGY:**
Think, Pair, Share

Find the materials you will need to teach this lesson plan at **hstry.is/mypart**.

Essential Questions

- **What is identity? What factors help shape who we are?**
- **How do our names relate to our identities?**

Overview

If each individual in the United States contributes to the nation's collective identity, then it makes sense to start a course exploring United States history by thinking about the individuals who comprise the nation.

According to American author Ralph Ellison, "It is through our names that we first place ourselves in the world. Our names, being the gift of others, must be made our own."[1] Indeed, when we meet someone new, our name is usually the first piece of information about ourselves that we share. It is often one of the first markers of our identity that others learn. In this lesson, we use names to introduce the concept of *identity* and the idea that each of our identities is the product of the relationship between the individual and society.

Students will then broaden their exploration of identity and consider the other factors that influence who we are as individuals. They will consider the parts of our identity that are given to us as well as the parts that we choose.

Activities

1. Consider the Relationship between Names and Identity

In this brief activity, students will read through a list of famous people who have changed their names. They will consider what choices these individuals were making about their identities when they changed their names.

- Share the reading Choosing Names. Ask students if they recognize any names from the list and if they have any ideas about why those individuals might have changed their names.

- Lead a discussion about the choice to change a name, using the questions below:

  - What reasons might people have for changing their names?

  - Do any of these name changes surprise you? Why?

1 Ralph Ellison, "Hidden Name and Complex Fate: A Writer's Experience in the United States," in *The Collected Essays of Ralph Ellison,* ed. John F. Callahan (New York: Modern Library, 2003), 192.

- Most of the people on this list are celebrities. Why do you think these people might have changed their names as they became more recognizable? What image might they have been trying to convey?

- The last two names on the list are of people who were emancipated from slavery after the Civil War. Why might they have chosen to change their names?

- How are names related to our personal histories? How might they be related to our national history?

- Are names the same as who we are? How much of you changes when your name changes?

2. Explore the Broader Identity a Name Represents

Students will continue their discussion of names by reflecting on how well they think their own name reflects who they are. They will then turn to other facets of identity, using the metaphor of an online search results page to think about the characteristics that make up who they are.

- Give students five minutes to journal about their names, using *one* of the following prompts:
  - I was given my name because . . .
  - I like/dislike my name because . . .
  - My name is/isn't a good fit for my personality because . . .
  - Describe a time when someone made an assumption about you because of your name.
  - Describe a time when your name affected your behavior.
- Provide students with copies of the reading Two Names, Two Worlds, and ask them to follow along as you read the text aloud.
- After reading the text, lead the class in a discussion based on the questions below. You might consider using the Think, Pair, Share strategy for the final question to offer students the opportunity to reflect more deeply.
  - What do you think Jonathan Rodríguez means when he uses the phrase "two names, two worlds"? What two worlds does his name represent?
  - Rodríguez says, "I'm not the typical kid from suburbia." He also says he is not a "smooth Latin cat." What does he mean by this? What evidence does he give to support his claims?
  - Who is Jonathan Rodríguez? Make a list of ten words he uses to describe himself.
- Introduce the concept of *identity*. Ask students: If names are one way we are given an identity and our identity is introduced to the rest of the world, how else do we become who we are?
- Ask students what they do when they want to know who or what someone or something "is." Someone will likely say, "Google it!" If not, introduce this idea, and then explain to students that you would like them to start thinking about

their own identities—"who they are"—by imagining what they would like to see among the results if they were to do an online search for their own name.

- As a class, brainstorm a list of what types of things determine someone's identity. Record these ideas, or categories, on the board. Examples might include:

  - Religious/spiritual affiliation
  - Culture, race, or ethnicity
  - Appearance/style
  - Language or nationality
  - Hobbies/interests
  - Gender
  - Sexual orientation
  - Beliefs and values
  - Group/organization/community membership
  - Personality traits

- With these and other categories in mind, ask students to create a mock online search results page for themselves in their journals. They can use the handout Online-Search Identity Chart to brainstorm ideas. On the page they create, instruct students to show what they would *like to see* in the results if they did an online search for themselves. Tell students that the "results" could include websites, images, videos, shopping profiles or reviews, and other types of pages or links. Consider creating a search results page for yourself as a model for your students, including images representing one of your interests, the website of a school you attended, and other basic information you are comfortable sharing.

- For homework, ask students to reflect on this activity using the following prompts:

  - How does your mock online search page answer the question, "Who am I?"
  - In what ways do you think this activity failed to capture aspects of your identity?
  - What characteristics do you think are important to your identity?

Choosing Names

The left column includes names you might recognize. The right column shows the birth name of each individual in the left column.

Chosen Name	Birth Name
Jay Z	Shawn Corey Carter
Lady Gaga	Stefani Joanne Angelina Germanotta
Jon Stewart	Jonathan Stuart Leibowitz
Mark Twain	Samuel Langhorne Clemens
Muhammad Ali	Cassius Clay
Kareem Abdul-Jabbar	Ferdinand Lewis Alcindor, Jr.
Nina Dobrev	Nikolina Konstantinova Dobreva
Jamie Foxx	Eric Marlon Bishop
Lorde	Ella Marija Lani Yelich-O'Connor
Charlie Sheen	Carlos Irwin Estévez
Chaz Bono	Chastity Bono
Nicki Minaj	Onika Tanya Maraj
Bruno Mars	Peter Gene Bayot Hernandez
Faith Hill	Audrey Perry
Lana Del Rey	Elizabeth Grant
Vin Diesel	Mark Vincent
Marilyn Monroe	Norma Jeane Mortenson
Caitlyn Jenner	Bruce Jenner
Dr. Seuss	Theodor Geisel
Dick Lewis Barnett	Dick Lewis Smith
Thomas Grant	Jeff Davis

Two Names, Two Worlds

In the poem below, student Jonathan Rodríguez reflects on how his name represents his identity.

Hi I'm Jon...........No — Jonathan

Wait — Jonathan Rodríguez

Hold on — Jonathan *Rodríguez*

My Name, Two names, two worlds

The duality of my identity like two sides of the same coin

With two worlds, there should be plenty of room

But where do I fit?

Where can I sit?

Is this seat taken? Or is that seat taken?

There never is quite enough room is there?

Two names, Two worlds

Where do I come from?

Born in the Washington heights of New York City

But raised in good ol' Connecticut

The smell of freshly mowed grass, autumn leaves

Sancocho, Rice and Beans

The sound from Billy Joel's Piano Keys

And the rhythm from *Juan Luis Guerra*

I'm from the struggle for broken dreams

Of false promises

Of houses with white picket fences

And 2.5 kids

The mountains and *campos de la Republica Dominicana*

And the mango trees

I'm not the typical kid from suburbia

Nor am I a smooth Latin cat

My head's in the clouds, my nose in a comic book

I get lost in the stories and art

I'm kinda awkward — so talkin' to the ladies is hard

I listen to *Fernando Villalona* and *Aventura* every chance I get,

But don't make me dance *Merengue, Bachata*

Or *Salsa* — I don't know the steps

I've learned throughout these past years

I am a mix of cultures, a mix of races

"Una Raza encendida,

Negra, Blanca y Taina"

You can find me in the parts of a song, *en una cancion*

You can feel my African Roots *en la Tambora*

My *Taino* screams *en la guira*

And the melodies of the lyrics are a reminder of my beautiful Spanish heritage

I am African, Taino and Spanish

A Fanboy, an athlete, a nerd, a student, an introvert

I'm proud to say: *Yo soy Dominicano*

I'm proud to say, I am me

I am beginning to appreciate that I am

Una bella mezcla

I am beginning to see that this world is also a beautiful mix

Of people, ideas and stories.

Is this seat taken?

Or is that seat taken?

Join me and take a seat,

Here we'll write our own stories[2]

2 Jonathan Rodríguez, untitled poem.

Online-Search Identity Chart

Answer the questions below to brainstorm ideas for your mock online search results page.

What are **two websites** that might say something about who you are or connect to your identity? List and describe them below.

Sketch and label **two images** that represent you or say something about who you are.

What is **one product, object, or piece of clothing** that represents something about yourself?

What is **one place** that is important to you and connects to a part of who you are?

Is there **a video** that represents something about yourself or that you feel connected to? It could be a viral video that relates to your sense of humor, a music video, or a TV or movie clip.

What is an **important date** (besides your birthday) that is meaningful to you and that relates to who you are?

3

Identity and Labels

Materials

IMAGE:
Still Calculus

VIDEO:
What Kind of
Asian Are You?

READING:
Still Me Inside

TEACHING STRATEGY:
Think, Pair, Share

TEACHING STRATEGY:
Fishbowl

Find the materials you will need to teach this lesson plan at **hstry.is/mypart**.

Essential Question

- **How do the labels and assumptions others make about us influence our identities?**

Overview

In the last lesson, students looked at different factors that can shape our identities. In this lesson, students will explore more deeply one particular influence on our identities: the assumptions others make about each of us and the labels they use to describe us.

Throughout our lives, people attach labels to us, and those labels reflect and affect how others think about our identities as well as how we think about ourselves. Labels are not always negative; they can reflect positive characteristics, set useful expectations, and provide meaningful goals in our lives. Often, however, the labels that we use to describe each other are the result of unfounded assumptions and stereotypes. We regularly apply labels to people whom we barely know or have never even met, and the same is done to us. Thus, for good or for bad, labels represent an influence on our identity that is often beyond our control.

The goals of this lesson are to provide students with the opportunity to explore some of the ways we use labels to identify each other and to consider the ways that those labels affect how others think about us, how we behave, and how we think about ourselves. By better understanding the effects of labels and stereotypes in their lives today, students may reach a better understanding of how similar ideas influenced Americans, and characters in American literature, in the past.

Activities

1. Reflect on How We Use Labels, Assumptions, and Stereotypes

In this opening activity, students will analyze a cartoon that comments on the calculations we make about each other, even during anonymous encounters on the street. Then students will explore the meaning of the terms *label*, *assumption*, and *stereotype*.

- Pass out or display the cartoon Street Calculus.

- Discuss students' first impressions of the image, beginning with the following questions:

  - What's happening in this image?

  - What do you notice about what each person is thinking in his thought bubble?

  - How are each of their thoughts similar? How are they different?

- Next, analyze the cartoon more deeply by having students discuss the following questions:

  - Do you think the situation depicted here is realistic? Do people use similar "lists" to make judgments about each other?

  - How aware do you think people are of the lists they make? When someone sees you walking down the street, what lists might they make about you? What lists do you sometimes make about others?

  - How might these lists shape choices people make (beyond greeting each other)? What would it take to change the lists people make about each other?

- Then introduce the terms *label*, *assumption*, and *stereotype*, using the definitions below. You might ask students to work together to write, share, and refine their own working definitions for these terms over the course of the lesson.

  - *Label*: A name, word, or phrase used to classify or categorize a person or thing (labels are often, but not always, inaccurate)

  - *Assumption*: Something that is accepted as true before one gathers any proof that it is so

  - *Stereotype*: An often incorrect assumption made about all of the members of a particular group

- Ask students how these terms could be used to describe the situation illustrated in the cartoon.

2. Analyze a Satire of Stereotypes

Students will watch a short video that satirizes the way we sometimes rely on stereotypes about race, ethnicity, and nationality to make assumptions about each other. Even when intentions are good, these types of assumptions have the power to complicate our interactions and to offend.

- Watch the video What Kind of Asian Are You? at hstry.is/mypart with your students. It is important, before sharing this video with the class, to help them understand the purpose of satire: to use exaggeration and humor to ridicule harmful behavior.

- As they are watching, ask students to make a T-chart, recording the man's actions on one side of the chart and the woman's responses to him on the other.

- After watching the video, lead a class discussion using the questions below.
  - What does the man want to know about the woman jogger? Why does he have such a difficult time asking his question clearly?
  - What characteristics does he associate with being Korean? Are his associations accurate?
  - How does the woman jogger respond? Do you think she is offended? What evidence does the video provide?
  - What point is she trying to make when she asks the man where he is from? Does he understand?
  - What effect did stereotypes have on this conversation? How can they complicate the interactions between people?
  - Describe a time when you found yourself in a similar situation. Were you the one making the assumptions, or were assumptions being made about you? How did you feel during that interaction? Did the interaction make you think about your identity differently? What might you do differently if the same situation happened again?

3. Consider the Effect Stereotypes Have on Us

Students will read the story of a young woman who, feeling the need for a change, cuts her hair, dyes it red, and gets an eyebrow piercing. Students will learn not only how these changes in her appearance led people to treat her differently—and sometimes hurtfully—but also how they taught her to be confident in who she truly is, despite the judgments and stereotypes applied to her by other people.

- Ask students to complete the following sentence, either in their journals or in pairs:

  Based only on my appearance, people would never expect that I _____.

- Then ask them to read Still Me Inside. Check their understanding of the text by leading a discussion, using the following questions as prompts:
  - What adjustments did Mai Goda make to change her appearance from "dork to punk"? Why does she say she decided to make these changes?
  - What do you think Goda means when she writes, "I felt somewhat obliged to appease the stereotype imposed on me"? What was the stereotype?
  - How did people's treatment of Goda change after she altered her appearance? What evidence does she give of people's new ideas about her identity?
  - What do you think Goda means when she says that she "performed well but felt awful" at her recital? What affected how she felt?
  - Why did Goda's conversation with her friend's dad make her feel like she had "won a battle"? How did this victory change her?

- What do you think Goda means when she says that she "traded one stereotype for another"? What is the "new" stereotype?

- Ask students to work individually to come up with three possible ways that Goda might complete this sentence:

  Based only on my appearance, people would never expect that I _____. Use the Think, Pair, Share strategy to briefly discuss students' responses.

- Close the activity by leading students in a Fishbowl discussion based on the following questions:

  - What do you think Goda means when she says she now enjoys proving the people who make assumptions about her wrong? How does she do this?

  - Did Goda's identity ever really change? What did change about her?

  - How do labels, assumptions, and stereotypes affect how other people identify each of us? How might labels, assumptions, and stereotypes affect how we think about ourselves?

- For homework, ask students to write a response in their journals to the following question (repeated from the class discussion). They can draw on ideas from the class discussion in their written responses:

  How do labels, assumptions, and stereotypes affect how other people identify each of us? How might labels, assumptions, and stereotypes affect how we think about ourselves?

Street Calculus

DOONESBURY © G. B. Trudeau. Reprinted with permission of UNIVERSAL UCLICK. All rights reserved.

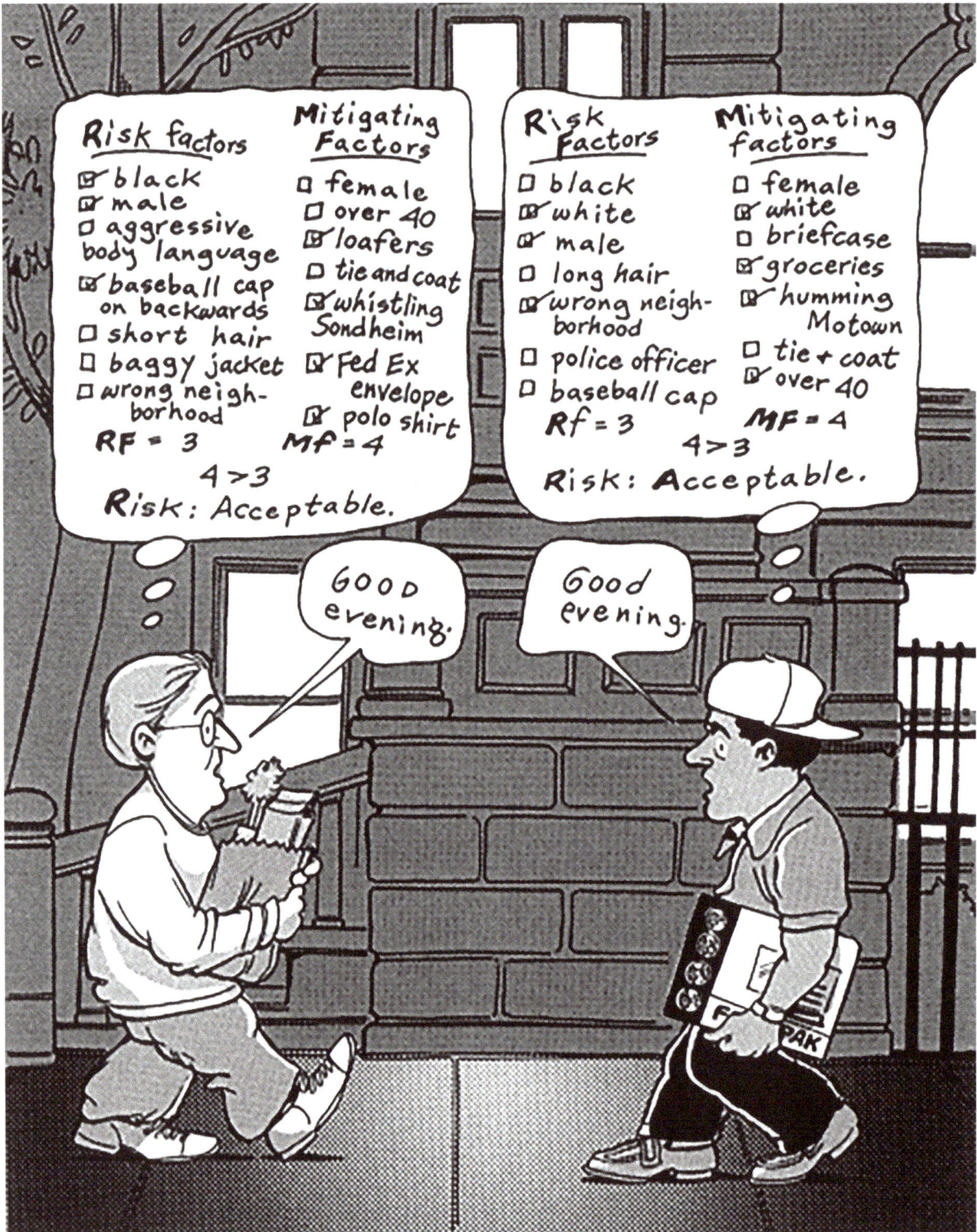

Garry Trudeau's cartoon from the *Doonesbury* comic strip comments on the calculations we make about one another.

Still Me Inside

Mai Goda describes how changing her appearance affected the way that others perceived her identity and how she thought about herself:

"I need a change!"

And so on that single whim, I cut my long black hair, streaked it bright red, and, to top it off, pierced my eyebrow. I had gone from dork to punk in a week, and as trivial as it seems, this transformation has had a great effect on my life.

As long as I can remember, I had always been a good girl. In school, I got decent grades and never was in trouble. At home, I tried not to give my parents too much grief. But more than that, I had the "look" of a good girl. People always stereotyped me as a quiet, studious, Asian girl. Friends' parents often asked if I played the violin or the piano. "No, the flute," I'd say, and they would nod, not surprised. Walking around with my long black hair over my face, I hid behind my stereotype. I felt somewhat obliged to appease the stereotype imposed on me.

Needless to say, heads turned the day I walked into school sporting a new, short, bright red hairdo. I enjoyed the reaction and attention I received from my friends and teachers. I didn't listen to my friends' warnings about people seeing me differently, people who frowned on a "rebellious punkster." After all, I was still the same person inside, so why should this change matter? I soon found out how naive I was.

One day, I was late for school and needed a pass from my vice principal. I was met by a surprisingly stern look. Writing one, his voice and stare were cold and condescending. Mistaking me for "one of those punk delinquents," he left me with a warning: "Don't make a habit of it." Had I come to school late a week before, my vice principal would have said nothing. I was not used to this discriminating treatment, and I felt angry, embarrassed, and somewhat defeated. Now every time I go to the mall, suspicious eyes follow me. Store clerks keep a cautious watch. But the worst was yet to come.

It was the night of our music recital for advanced students. For weeks, I had prepared my piece, and I was excited. The room was packed with parents waiting to hear their children. But, as soon as I walked into the room, all attention was focused on my head. As I sat waiting my turn, I felt the critical eyes of the parents.

I performed well but felt awful. Afterward, I still saw those disapproving looks as they walked out with their children. I even overheard a friend being lectured on how she shouldn't color her hair or pierce her face to become a "punk like Mai." Once again, I was ready to go home feeling angry when my friend's father stopped me.

"You were very good tonight. At first I didn't recognize you," he said, looking at my head.

"Oh yes, I look very different from last time, don't I?"

"Well, you played even better than last year. Look forward to hearing you again."

I went home feeling good, as if I had finally won a battle. Now the stern look of the vice principal, the suspicious stares of the store clerks, and the disapproving eyes of my friends' mothers didn't bother me. I was still the same person inside, punk or not. There was nothing wrong with me; it was the other judgmental people who had the problem. I regained my confidence.

I still get looks and the stares, but it doesn't upset me. In a way, I traded in one stereotype for another, but this time I enjoy proving them wrong. People are surprised to see me getting good grades and applying to good colleges. They're surprised to hear me play the flute so well. And they are absolutely shocked to see me standing in front of the football field, red hair shining in the sun, conducting the marching band.

As for my red hair, I re-dye it occasionally to keep it bright, burning red. It seems to give me the power to fight against stereotypes forced on me and gives me the confidence that I never had before.[1]

---

1 Mai Goda, "Still Me Inside," in *Chicken Soup for the Teen Soul: Real-Life Stories by Real Teens,* ed. Jack Canfield, Mark Victor Hansen, Stephanie H. Meyer, and John Myer (Backlist, LLC, 2012), 261–263.

LESSON 4
Identity and Choices

Find the materials you will need to teach this lesson plan at **hstry.is/mypart**.

Materials

IMAGE:
Our Kind of People

READING:
Creating Ourselves Online and in "Real Life"

READING:
Computer Keyboard

READING:
Chameleon

TEACHING STRATEGY:
Gallery Walk

Essential Questions

- **What choices do we make about our own identities?**
- **How can our choices influence how others see us?**
- **How can our choices influence how we understand ourselves?**

Overview

The last two lessons of this unit demonstrated how outside factors such as names, labels, and assumptions can influence identity. One goal of this lesson is to help students become more self-aware and realize that they have the opportunity to make choices about who they are. Sometimes the choices a person makes, consciously or unconsciously, can affect how others perceive that person. Students will consider how choices—like deciding what to wear in the morning, how to style themselves, or how to present themselves on social media—can emphasize some aspects of their identities while minimizing or hiding others.

Sometimes others react to us based on choices we make, and the reactions of others can affect our future choices. This feedback loop can be observed perhaps most plainly in the ways that we create and revise our identities online. When we first join a social media platform, we pick and choose the parts of our identities to share in our profiles and postings, and if we do not receive the comments and "likes" that we are looking for, we revise. In this lesson, by examining the thought processes of others who are negotiating identity online, students can better reflect on their own experiences and also make connections to the ways that they manage their identities in "real life."

Another goal of this lesson is to prompt students to explore the idea of choosing to follow personal interests, for it is often through pursuits we feel passionate about that we are able to break free from the identity feedback loop described above. When we are able to lose ourselves (or "find ourselves," as it were) in a topic or activity that speaks deeply to us, the perceptions others make about us often matter at least a little bit less and we are able to present ourselves maybe in a more accurate form.

Activities

1. Reflect on the Relationship between Our Choices and Others' Perceptions

Students begin this lesson by reflecting on the various, seemingly mundane choices they make in their daily routines and how these are influenced by what other people might think about them. This activity helps to illustrate how the opinions of others (or, at least, our perception of their opinions) can influence the way we choose to represent ourselves.

- Give students a few minutes to write down their school-day morning routine in their journals. You might want to provide an example by sharing a sample routine (yours or the one below):
  - Wake up
  - Use the bathroom
  - Eat breakfast
  - Brush teeth
  - Shower
  - Style hair
  - Get dressed
  - Put on accessories
  - Put on shoes
  - Pack bookbag, backpack, purse, etc.
  - Leave for school

- Then instruct students to indicate, on a scale of one to ten, how much other people's opinions matter when they make choices such as those about what to wear and how to style themselves in the morning. They should put a number between one and ten next to each step of their morning routine. Explain the scale:

    1 = choice based solely on personal desires and wishes

    10 = choice based entirely on what other people think

- After students have had a chance to reflect on their routines, use the questions below to lead the class in a short discussion to identify some of the instances in which they—consciously or subconsciously—make choices that might affect how people perceive them.
  - Which choices do you make in your morning routine that might affect people's opinions of you? What assumptions might someone make about your identity based on these choices?
  - What might happen if you made different choices one morning? How could making a different choice in your hairstyle, fashion, or another aspect of your routine affect how people look at you?

2. Analyze the Connection between Appearances and Assumptions

In this activity, students explore images from Bayeté Ross Smith's "Our Kind of People" photography exhibit and think about how the choices individuals make about the clothes they wear can influence how others perceive them.

- Before you start, prepare for this activity by taking these steps:
  - Visit the website for artist Bayeté Ross Smith's online photography exhibit (see bayeterosssmith.com). This exhibit includes six sets of photographs. Each series consists of the same person photographed six times, each time in a completely different outfit from his or her own wardrobe. The power of each series comes from the fact that one might draw very different conclusions about the identity of the same person depending on which photograph of him or her one is viewing.
  - One set of individual images are provided in this lesson (see Our Kind of People, images 1–6). Print out each of the six photographs of that person on separate sheets of paper.
- Divide your class into six small groups, and provide each group with one of the printed photographs. Each group should have a different photograph, but do not tell the students that these are all photographs of the same person.
- Instruct each group to brainstorm and write down a list of labels or assumptions someone might make about the person in the photo, answering the question: What assumptions might someone make (regardless of what this person intended to convey) about this person's identity?
- At this point, have groups leave their photos on a desk or table and have students walk around the room to see the other photos. It will likely be a surprise to all the groups to see the same individual in different outfits and with different labels and assumptions assigned to him. After students return to their seats, conduct a class discussion, using the following questions as prompts:
  - Why did each group have different labels for photos of the same person?
  - How do we use labels to understand each other? When might those labels be incorrect or incomplete?
  - Where do the labels and stereotypes we apply to others come from?
  - All of the subject's clothing came from his own wardrobe. Does this surprise you? Why or why not?
  - How does clothing allow people to emphasize certain parts of their identities? In what ways does it allow people to hide other aspects of who they are?
  - These images are part of a larger work by an artist named Bayeté Ross Smith, titled "Our Kind of People." What message do you think the artist was trying to convey by creating this project?

- You might want to share this statement by Bayeté Ross Smith describing the choices he made when creating this exhibit:

  > The "Our Kind Of People" series examines how clothing, ethnicity and gender affect our ideas about identity, personality and character. The subjects in this work are dressed in clothing from their own wardrobes. The outfits are worn in a style and fashion similar to how that person would wear them in daily life. I have kept the lighting and facial expressions the same in each photograph, changing only the clothing and race. Devoid of any context for assessing the personality of the individual in the photograph, the viewer projects her or his own cultural biases on each photograph. These images may be presented in a series, grouped together by the subject, or mixed together, with images of the various subjects next to each other.

3. Compare and Contrast Online and "Real Life" Identity

This activity includes excerpts from interviews with teens, conducted by the Pew Research Center, about how young people share their identities online. Students will use the excerpts found in the reading Creating Ourselves Online and in "Real Life" to think about the ways they portray their identities online and how those online identities relate to who they are in "real life."

- Before you start, prepare for this activity by taking the following steps:
  - Familiarize yourself with the Gallery Walk teaching strategy and gather paper to use. Chart paper or paper larger than 8.5" by 11" is best.
  - Read through the excerpts in the reading Creating Ourselves Online and in "Real Life," and choose five to six to use with your students. Tape each excerpt you choose on a separate piece of chart paper and post them around the room.

- Tell students that after thinking about outward appearances, they will now be thinking about how they represent themselves online. Ask students to make a T-chart in their journals. Have them write the heading "In Real Life" on the left-hand column. Then ask them to make a list of all the labels and assumptions a total stranger might make about them based on how they look and act "in real life."

- Next, have students write the heading "Social Media" on the right-hand column. Under that heading, they should list all the labels and assumptions a stranger might make about them based *only* on their social media persona.

- Give students two minutes to respond to the following prompt in their journals:

  > When I look at the two lists, I notice that my "real life" and "online" identities are _____ because _____.

- Introduce the idea that, just as we choose every morning how to represent ourselves with our clothing or hairstyle, every time we open our Facebook, Instagram, Twitter, or other social media accounts, we make choices about how we represent ourselves online. Explain that the profiles we create, the comments we make, and the posts of others that we "like" all contribute to an online identity that is often similar to—but sometimes very different from—our identity in "real life."

- Post the "big papers" with interview excerpts around the room. Give students 10 to 15 minutes to participate in a silent written discussion about their excerpt, following the Gallery Walk teaching strategy. Ask students to read the excerpts and circle places where the speaker talks about choices he or she made about his or her online identity.

- After the silent portion of the discussion, lead the class in a conversation to explore the themes that emerged during the activity. Use the following questions:

  - What were some of the concerns that each speaker had about how his or her identity was expressed online?

  - How did other people's opinions of them affect what they chose to share or not share? Where would their choices fit on the one-to-ten scale?

    1 = choice based solely on personal desires and wishes

    10 = choice based entirely on what other people think

4. Discuss What It Means to "Find Your Voice"

In this activity, students read two texts. In the first, Computer Keyboard, Gerard reflects on how he developed a love of taking apart gadgets and equipment to learn how they work. In the second story, Chameleon, David recalls a time when he bought shoes to fit in with his high school friends, and he describes his surprise when his new shoes did not command the reception he expected. The texts together help students consider the ways that individuals can find their voices as well as the courage to listen to their voices, despite what others say to or about them.

- Divide the class into pairs. Give each pair one copy of each reading; one student will read David's story and the other will read Gerard's story.

- Ask each pair to imagine a conversation between David and Gerard, in which they discuss some of the following questions:

  - What are your interests? What draws you to those interests?

  - How have people in your life reacted to your interests?

  - Have you ever felt different from the crowd? When and how?

  - What advice would you give a high school student about trying to fit in?

  - What advice would you give a high school student trying to decide how to represent him or herself to friends and family?

- In the remaining class time, or for homework, ask students to respond to one of the following prompts in their journals:

  - Describe a time in your life when your concerns about how you would be perceived by others affected a decision you made, either online or in "real life."

  - Do you relate more to Gerard's or David's story? Why?

- Who are the people with whom you can be and show your truest self? Who are you when you are with them? In what ways do they give you confidence to just be you?

- What are you passionate about? How do the things you are passionate about help shape who you are?

Extension

- If you want to explore more themes about the role that images, assumptions, and social media play in shaping how we think about and act toward ourselves and others, see the lesson #IfTheyGunnedMeDown from the unit Facing Ferguson: News Literacy in a Digital Age at hstry.is/mypart.

Our Kind of People (image 1)

Bayeté Ross Smith, *Our Kind of People*, Part Three, 2010

Our Kind of People (image 2)

Bayeté Ross Smith, *Our Kind of People*, Part Three, 2010

Our Kind of People (image 3)

Bayeté Ross Smith, *Our Kind of People, Part Three, 2010*

Our Kind of People (image 4)

Bayeté Ross Smith, *Our Kind of People*, Part Three, 2010

Our Kind of People (image 5)

Bayeté Ross Smith, *Our Kind of People*, Part Three, 2010

Our Kind of People (image 6)

Bayeté Ross Smith, *Our Kind of People*, Part Three, 2010

Creating Ourselves Online and in "Real Life"

In 2012, the Pew Research Center surveyed young people to learn about how they represented themselves online. The following are excerpts from interviews Pew conducted with teenagers.

1. Female (age 14): "OK, so I do post a good amount of pictures, I think. Sometimes it's a very stressful thing when it comes to your profile picture. Because one should be better than the last, but it's so hard. So . . . I will message [my friends] a ton of pictures. And be like which one should I make my profile? And then they'll help me out. And that kind of takes the pressure off me. And it's like a very big thing."

2. Female (age 14): "I think I wouldn't [become Facebook friends with my teachers]. Just because I'm such a different person online. I'm more free. And obviously, I care about certain things, but I'm going to post what I want. I wouldn't necessarily post anything bad that I wouldn't want them to see, but it would just be different. And I feel like in the classroom, I'm more professional [at] school. I'm not going to scream across the room oh my God, I want to dance! Or stuff like that. So I feel if they saw my Facebook they would think differently of me. And that would probably be kind of uncomfortable. So I probably would not be friends with them."

3. Male (age 18): "Yeah, I go to church and all, so I don't want to post certain things because I don't want the preacher looking at my Facebook. Because I go to church with her. So then if she sees me, yeah, baby, and yeah. I feel like it does affect the way you use social [media]. You have that respect for something or for a group that you're into or anything, like . . . yourself, because maybe that's who you are, but at the same time, you love that group and you never want to disrespect them. So at that point, I feel like it does affect you. Sometimes affecting you doesn't always mean negatively. It can sometime[s] be positively, you know?"

4. Male (age 18): "Yeah, I have some teachers who have connections that you might want to use in the future, so I feel like you always have an image to uphold. Whether I'm a person that likes to have fun and go crazy and go all out, but I don't let people see that side of me because maybe it changes the judgment on me. So you post what you want people to think of you, basically."

5. Female (age 16): "I deleted it [my Facebook account] when I was 15, because I think it [Facebook] was just too much for me with all the gossip and all the cliques and how it was so important to be—have so many friends—I was just like it's too stressful to have a Facebook, if that's what it has to take to stay in contact with just a little people. It was just too strong, so I just deleted it. And I've been great ever since."

6. Female (age 16): "And our SRO [School Resource Officer], he has information. He can see anything that we do, basically, because he's part of the police department. And so he's talked to my friends and I before. And he was like, anything you do, I can pull up. So if y'all tweet about a party, while you're there, just don't be surprised when it gets busted."[1]

1 Mary Madden and Amanda Lenhart, "What teens said about social media, privacy, and online identity," Pew Research Center, May 21, 2013, http://www.pewinternet.org/2013/05/21/what-teens-said-about-social-media-privacy-and-online-identity/.

Computer Keyboard

What does it mean to find yourself? Sometimes we find our passions, our voices, in the objects around us. Gerard K., an immigrant from the Democratic Republic of Congo, explains:

When I was young, I loved to open up my father's equipment, like his remote, phone, and camera, to see what was inside. I wanted to know what made them work. I could see my father's face. He was so frustrated, shaking his head no. He would pull my ears and yell at me, "Don't open my equipment anymore!"

"But Dad, I just want to learn, to know how it works," I would say, touching my ear and crying.

"Don't open it if you don't know how to fix it back," said my dad, and he took his hand off my ear. My ear felt so hot that I went in the kitchen, opened the refrigerator, took cold water, and put my ear inside the bowl. I think my father was asking himself, "Why doesn't my son listen, he thinks he will learn how to be an engineer by destroying my equipment?" I don't blame him. The problem was, he didn't understand technology.

It was very easy for me to find gadgets in the Democratic Republic of Congo. People threw their electronics and cables that didn't work anymore in a big trash hole behind their houses. I could hear the noise of the rats eating cables, and who knows, maybe they spoke in their language, wondering, "What do we have for dinner today?" One day, I found a small red light in a toy car. An idea popped into my mind to create a small antenna, using a candle and a toothpick. The project took two days.

"How come you can do more things than other kids of your age?" my mother would say.

"I don't know, maybe it's just because I love to do it," I said, looking at my antenna.

One afternoon, I was so tired of staying in the house all day without doing anything. I decided to go see my friends and I proposed to them that they walk with me. There was a small street on the left side of our avenue. There were a lot of dirty plastic bags, sandals, and shoes everywhere. It smelled like rotten food and nobody liked to pass through. Rumors were that people were killed there. We were passing nearby and something caught my attention. I didn't know what it was. I stopped walking, and looked at the object again, curious to know. My friends stopped, too. They asked me, *"C'est quoi le probleme?"*

"Everything is okay, just wait for me," I replied.

As I walked down that dangerous street, getting closer and closer, my heart beat very fast. I wondered what I was doing. I walked until I reached the place. I touched the black thing and saw that it was a strong plastic, dirty keyboard with no screen. "Yes!" I said, jumping around like Kirkou. My two friends were impressed to see me dancing around because of a keyboard. "I am going home right now," I said, laughing. My friends must have been thinking, "This dude will never change."

When I got home, I cleaned my keyboard with a t-shirt till all the dust came off. My brother came in the bedroom and saw me pressing the keyboard without any screen or mouse. *"Tu es fou,"* he said, shaking his head. Even though they thought I was crazy, their reaction didn't change my passion.

Today I can open a microwave, a computer, and even a TV. I have become like an advisor. My dad takes me to Best Buy so I can show him what to buy. I tell him to get old computers, so even if they break, we can always replace them with new parts. I can do this for him because I have never stopped learning. That is one thing that I love about myself.[2]

---

2 Gerard Kasemba, "Computer Keyboard," in *I Want You to Have This: A Collection of Objects and Their Stories from Around the World,* written by eleventh graders from Boston International High School (Boston, MA: 826 Boston, 2013), 44.

Chameleon

Our desire to fit in sometimes influences the choices me make. Here, David L. describes what happened once when he went to great lengths to fit in.

High school students are a lot like chameleons. They love to blend into their surroundings. Walk down the halls of a high school and you will see exactly that: students trying to fit in. Similar to chameleons, high school students do it for the same reason—survival. Being singled out is a dangerous thing. In a place where reputation defines you, having anything jeopardize that reputation can prove dreadful. In my freshman year, I was in a group of friends who loved to talk about shoes. Our conversations consisted of shoes, Call of Duty, shoes, girls, shoes, shoes, and school. The more they talked about it, the more I saw sneaker trends everywhere I went. It wasn't long until I figured out that all the "popular" kids had the most expensive sneakers, more specifically Jordans. Looking down at my plain, worn-out shoes, I knew I was no match. How could I expect to survive high school if I had nothing to show on my feet?

That night, I scrolled through page after page of Jordans. Different designs, different colors, but all well over $100. Which ones were cool? What designs were best? Didn't that one senior wear these? He got a lot of attention at school. Maybe I should get the same. Nah, probably not. Maybe these? An hour into my search, I finally saw the pair I wanted—the Royal Blue 10s. This pair not only had my favorite color schemes (blue, white and silver) but they were, more importantly, "cool" enough for me to be recognized and accepted. In a jungle of trendsetters I was the chameleon trying to blend in. I woke up at 7 a.m. on a chilly March Saturday morning. It was the day the Royal Blue 10s were being released.

I waited patiently outside the Champs store for two hours. All the guys around me had $100+ shoes. They discussed the newest releases and the sneaker trades as I stood there awkwardly in my $60 Nikes. I felt out of place, and even if I could fit in, I slowly realized I didn't want to. My thoughts were interrupted by the sound of a door opening. All heads turned toward the employee coming out of the store. Within 30 seconds, those outside in the cold jam-packed into the small store, dollar bills waving in the air. Stealthily sneaking toward the front, I got the shoes, paid, and quickly left with a vibrant smile on my face. Whatever doubt I had before had gone.

That Monday, I wore the shoes for the first time. As I slipped them on, I could feel the soft sole press against the bottom of my foot. The new shoe smell flew up my nose. I could just imagine the look of awe on everyone's face, the compliments I would get, and most of all, the recognition. With a delicate hand, I wiped off a minor smudge on the side of the right one. A smile hit my face as I laced them up. Perfect.

There was a hop to my step that day and my head was held just a little bit higher. Looking around, I met everyone in the eye expecting to catch one of them staring at my shoes. First period passed. Nothing. Second period passed. Same thing. No compliments or anything. By lunch, I embraced my disappointment. I had imagined that I would be transformed into a new light, but as soon as I stepped through the school door I was still the same old freshman I was the week before. How could that be? I had the Jordans and everything. Were they really worth $160 and two hours of my time? Not once did I ask myself whether I truly wanted the pair. The shoes didn't represent who I was, but I had imagined the shoes would help create a better me. What I failed to realize, however, is that when chameleons try to avoid being singled out, they don't fit into their surroundings. They disappear.[3]

3 David Lopera, "Chameleon," in *It's Not the Stone that Brings You Strength* (Boston, MA: 826 Boston, 2014), 77–79.

5 LESSON
Connecting to the Past

Materials

READING:
What Are You?

READING:
The Wooden Shoes

VIDEO:
The Wooden Shoes

READING:
Black Belt

READING:
A Strength of My Neighborhood

READING:
Family Names

TEACHING STRATEGY:
Jigsaw

TEACHING STRATEGY:
Think, Pair, Share

Find the materials you will need to teach this lesson plan at **hstry.is/mypart**.

Essential Questions

- **To what extent do we inherit or receive our identities? How do the legacies of older generations influence our identities?**
- **How is each of us connected to the past? How has history influenced who each of us is today?**

Overview

This lesson asks students to consider the impact of both family legacies and the broader sweep of history on their identities. As journalist Maria Hinojosa stated in the first lesson of this unit, we all have stories of how we got "here": individual stories, family stories. For better or for worse, we owe at least part of who we are to the choices our families and other important people in our lives have made, as well as the choices made by even older generations. These choices create for each of us a kind of legacy that influences our identities, our circumstances, and, in turn, the choices we make. Yet all of these choices, including the ones we make today, are made within a larger historical context. When we consider the legacies we have received from our individual families, we might also find personal connections to the history of our communities, our nation, and the world. Either way, this examination can bring us to a deeper understanding of who we are.

The exploration of legacies and personal connections to history in this lesson prepares students to think about the impact of history on the identity of a nation in the next lesson. The identity of a nation is certainly affected by the legacies of those who were part of that nation's past; their choices, their collaborations, their conflicts all shape the identity of the nation in the present day.

Activities

1. Reflect on "Object Memories"

Several of the resources in this lesson that discuss legacies relate to objects that remind people of their individual or family histories. Even if we do not have those items in our possession today, we can all think of specific and tangible things (a toy, a photograph, a book, etc.) that feel closely related to our identities.

- Read aloud to students the following paragraph from the essay "Object Memories" by an author named Tova:

    I don't like throwing things away. By "things" I don't mean chairs, or blankets, or pants that are too small—I mean boxes of collected scraps and objects from all sorts of different events and times of my life . . . What seems like pieces of trash to everyone else are objects that hold all of my stories . . . It's not so much the fear of letting the thing itself go, but rather a terrible fear of losing whatever time or memory the object has come to signify. . . .

    Most of me understands that forgetting is just how life works. . . . Most of me is fine with this. It's nice to know that I don't have to remain tied to the identity and opinions of the person I was three years ago and four years ago and 10 years ago. But, while most of me happily accepts the changes and replacements each year brings, a tiny part of me rejects them. This tiny fearful part of me rebels against the displacing and replacing of memory and identity . . . [1]

    Explain to students that Tova goes on to describe dried roses, a collection of notebooks, and a shoebox from her past that all connect meaningfully to her identity.

- Ask students to respond in their journals to the following prompt:

    Write about an object or some other tangible item that you have (or had) that connects to your personal or family history. What is the "thing," and what does it mean to you?

- Optionally, you might ask for volunteers to share parts of their journal reflections. You might also ask students to bring in their objects the next day.

2. Explore Identity and Legacy

In this activity, students will analyze four readings in which individuals describe objects, places, and other personal items that represent to them important parts of their identities and their personal histories. Students will use these readings as a springboard for reflecting on the things in their lives that have meaning because of the way they represent their personal or family histories.

- Working in groups, students will use the Jigsaw strategy to read and analyze four short essays about the influence of the past on identity. Divide the class into groups of three or four, and provide each group with one of the following readings:

    - What Are You?: While growing up in Canada, Anna searches for a way to relate to her Indian heritage. Eventually she moves beyond the labels and stereotypes about Indian culture and finds a deeper connection with her grandfather, Poppy.

    - The Wooden Shoes: Cassania, a 17-year-old Boston high school student, tells the story of a pair of wooden shoes her grandfather gave to her as a

1 Tova, "Object Memories" (April 13, 2016), *Rookie,* issue 56.

gift. While she initially did not appreciate the shoes, she writes about how they came to represent to her the challenges and sacrifices her grandfather made for the family in Haiti, the Dominican Republic, and the United States. (Note that students assigned this reading can also watch the accompanying five-minute video The Wooden Shoes at hstry.is/mypart, following along in the reading as they watch.)

- Black Belt: Marc, an 18-year-old Boston high school student, reminds us that legacies are not left to us only by older generations. Marc was raised and mentored by his older brother, Jacky, until Jacky's death. Marc writes about the karate black belt that Jacky gave him and reflects on the enormous impact Jacky made on his identity by teaching him to believe in himself.

- A Strength of My Neighborhood: Juan writes about his neighborhood in Los Angeles and how it helps him feel connected to the culture and traditions of his family's "old world" heritage in Mexico.

- In their groups, ask students to read aloud their assigned reading together. Then have them discuss the following questions:

  - What connects the author to his or her past? Is it an object or something else?

  - What does that "thing" represent to the author? What does it remind this person of about themselves, their identity, or their personal history?

  - Students should then sketch the "thing" in their journals and write on it or next to it what it represents about the past to the author.

- Shuffle students into new groups. Each member of each new group should have read and analyzed a different story in the previous step. In these new groups, each student will summarize reading and share the images they created in their original group.

3. Connect to History

In this activity, students will think about how names can represent both identities and history. In the lesson Identity and Names, students considered the extent to which their names represent their identities. In this activity, they will read how one man learned more about the history behind his family name, and how that history connected him to his family's legacy in the United States.

- Pass out the reading Family Names. Read it aloud with the class, and then have students use the Think, Pair, Share strategy to respond to the following questions:

  - What did Macky Alston learn about his name?

  - Why do you think it felt like a secret?

- After groups have completed their discussions, share the following quotation from African American writer James Baldwin:

  > History is not the past. It is the present. We carry our history with us. We are our history.[2]

- Lead a brief class discussion analyzing the Baldwin quotation, beginning with the following questions:
  - What does Baldwin mean? In what ways might the past still be present in our lives?
  - Would Macky Alston agree with Baldwin? Why or why not?
- Finally, ask students to reflect on the following questions in their journals:
  - How much do you know about the history behind your family name and the way it connects you to the world?
  - If you decided to explore your family and its history, what places would you visit? Whom would you interview? What questions would you ask?
  - How might the answers you get help you understand something about what happened in the past?

4. Illustrate "Object Memories"

In the opening activity, students wrote about an object that connects them to their personal or family history. To close this lesson, they will return to that object and reconsider the ways in which it represents the past to them.

> Ask students to return to the objects they wrote about at the beginning of the lesson. Before the end of class, or for homework, ask each student to sketch (or visually represent in another way) the object they wrote about and write on it or next to it what it represents to them about their past. (Some students may wish to choose a different object than they wrote about originally.)

Extension

Consider having the class or small groups combine their visual representations from the "Object Memories" activity into a mosaic representing the identity of the class. Use the Flag of Faces from the first lesson as a model of a "mosaic of images."

Ask the class to make observations about their class creation and infer what it suggests about the class's collective identity. Ask students what the creation says about both the identity of individual students and their group identity as a class of students studying history together.

---

2 James Baldwin, *The Cross of Redemption: Uncollected Writings,* ed. Randall Kenan (New York: Vintage, 2011), 154.

What Are You?

Canadian writer Anna Fitzpatrick reflects on how she relates to her grandfather and her family history:

As with any of my Poppy's stories, I had to press him to learn the details behind his tattoos. They were easy to miss, a muddled *s.d.* on his left forearm and an even shakier *s.p.* on his right, in faded ink that barely stood out against his weathered skin.

"They are my initials" was his answer the first time I asked him about them, when I was about eight. . . . "Satya Dev was the name I was born with," he said. "When I was a boy—eight or nine—a man with a business on the side of the road asked if I wanted to get my initials tattooed, and I thought, Why not? Not long after, my father changed my name to Satya Pal." He went and got those letters tattooed as well.

With each explanation came more questions. How did his father change his name? Was there a ceremony? A ritual? Did he tell him why he changed it?

"No. He just started calling me Satya Pal one day" . . .

My mother—Poppy's daughter—didn't even know the story behind his tattoos until I asked him in front of her. . . . Most people who knew him knew only the most basic details of his life: He left India in his 20s to work in England as a marine engineer, and met my Nana in a small English town. They moved to Calcutta, where my mom and her brothers were born, then emigrated to Canada, where I was born and have lived my entire life. . . .

Compared with my Poppy's childhood, mine was pretty dull. I grew up in a fairly multicultural neighborhood where having parents from a different place wasn't that big a deal. Sundays we would go to my grandparents' house and eat tandoori chicken and dal. There'd usually be an Indian movie playing on TV, but the only person watching would be my English grandmother. My mom took me to a Hindu temple once when I was very young, I suppose as a way to connect me to my culture. . . .

Physically, I don't look very Indian. My skin is light, with yellowish undertones. I have dark, bushy hair and eyebrows, and muddled blue eyes. From middle school on, curious classmates would ask, "So, what are you?"—the question that every mixed-race person is all too familiar with. I had a hard time answering. To call myself "brown" felt like a farce. I was born and raised in Canada. My dad is white, and my mother is from India but has completely assimilated into Western culture. Claiming brownness felt like inserting myself into a culture that wasn't my own—and this was long before I knew what the word *appropriation* meant. Calling myself "white" felt equally wrong, like dipping a paintbrush into a pot of white paint and streaking it over our family portrait until it erased my Poppy's stories, my mom's childhood, and the family members lost during the violent partition of India in 1947, creating a blank slate onto which could be projected a picture of quintessential Caucasian girlhood.

So I usually answered "What are you?" with the simple, safe, monosyllabic "Mixed" . . .

As I got older, I started to read more about identity politics and became protective of—and sometimes defensive about—my Indian background. With a name like Fitzpatrick, I never had to explain to anybody that I had some Irish ancestors, despite the fact that the last one came three generations before me. It could be taken for granted that, as a light-skinned, English-speaking person living in Canada, I must have some European blood. But I felt like I had to almost prove my Indianness. "You don't *look* Indian," said one girl in my eighth grade social studies class when I was working on a family-tree project, as if I was trying to dupe the class. . . .

I tried . . . to be "Indian." I took my cues from Western movies with Indian characters, like *Bend It Like Beckham*. . . . I would look to my Indian friends, whose parents had immigrated later in their lives, and who still had a grasp on their parents' language, or practiced Hinduism. When I became a vegetarian, I started to cook more curries. I listened to popular Indian music and started teaching myself Hindi with books from the library. While I developed a genuine love for all these things, it still felt hollow to distill an entire culture down to food, music, and language, and my superficial knowledge of all three. Reading texts on Hinduism, or the history of India's independence, I felt like . . . an outsider . . .

My grandfather and I started talking all the time when I was in my late teens. . . . My understanding of India wasn't shaped by . . . songs on my iPod or the mutter paneer on my stove . . . but by the relationship I forged with a family member . . .

After Poppy died, I celebrated my 23rd birthday. . . . My aunt wanted to go to the Hindu temple [and she] took us to each shrine, explaining the importance of every deity. . . . *This is my history, this is my family, this is my identity*. But I couldn't feel it—not there in the temple.

Later that day, my brother drove my sister and me downtown and dropped us off in front of a tattoo parlor ("It's your birthday present," my siblings explained). I showed the man behind the counter the . . . picture I had taken of my Poppy's forearms . . . [and] within moments I was sitting in a leather chair, gripping my sister's hand, as the ink-filled needle scratched an *s.d.* and an *s.p.* into my own skin.[3]

3   Anna Fitzpatrick, "What Are You?" (June 13, 2013), *Rookie*, issue 22, http://www.rookiemag.com/2013/06/what-are-you.

The Wooden Shoes

Cassania, a 17-year-old student in Boston who emigrated from Haiti after the earthquake there in 2010, wrote this story about the legacy embodied in of a pair of wooden shoes.

On January 12, 2010, an earthquake devastated the small island of Haiti. As the earth shook, people were running all over the streets, trying to find a secure place. I saw a house that had fallen into pieces and plenty of people lying dead on the streets—some without a head, arm, or leg. My grandma and I had to leave quickly, so we only had time to take the most important things. I grabbed our cell phones. She grabbed a pair of yellow wooden shoes, but then we decided to leave them in the next room, and we went off.

Two days after my tenth birthday, April 23, my grandfather gave me a pair of yellow wooden shoes. They were the weirdest shoes that I'd ever seen in my life. Aside from being yellow, they were enormous, shiny, and had large beaks. They also had flower designs on each side. They were very clean, therefore they always had the smell of a newly bought thing. At first, I hated that pair of shoes because they weren't my style and they were not the kind of birthday gift that I wanted. When he gave me the shoes, I accepted them, but it was not a sincere acceptance. I threw them under my bed and went off. How could a ten-year-old girl love a weird pair of yellow shoes? However, my grandfather never gave up. He was extremely persistent and wanted me to know the story behind them, which he was truly proud of. I did not know how significant the shoes were until I sat down and listened to all the struggles that he had to go through.

My grandfather Fanis Julson was born in the Dominican Republic. When he was just about seventeen years old, his parents and he moved to Haiti. This wasn't easy for him because he had to leave his friends and family behind, and he had to start adapting himself to a new culture, a new life. But

Grandpa Fanis was strong enough to carry his own weight. He was extremely strict with his family, but when he was with his friends he was eager to have fun. He was compassionate, loved without limits, and appreciated even the smallest things in life. Since I was a little girl, people have always compared me to him because we share the same characteristics. He could never trick my mom or me, his own blood.

My grandpa used to live in the rural areas of Haiti. There was always a big lack of money in the family. About a year or so after my grandpa got married to my grandmother, Leonie Camille, things weren't going as well as he planned. Their three children were getting seriously sick. So everyday for fifteen years, he worked two jobs. He has worked as a salesman, but his primary job was being a comedian. He enjoyed entertaining people. He used to wake up at 5:00 a.m. every day, put his wooden shoes on, then go tell stories or act in a play for a certain family. Even when he got paid little money, it was enough to put food on the table for his family.

After hearing this intriguing story, I broke into tears. I went to my grandpa and gave him the biggest hug ever. He worked so hard to provide for the woman that he loved.

I decided to use these shoes for my project. I was so excited. I went home and asked Grandma about the shoes, but she did not answer me. She looked as scared as my cat Mickey whenever he hears a thunderstorm. She has an innocent look, whenever she does anything wrong, you always know because she looks nervous. Having the feeling that she didn't hear me, I asked her the question once again, and that's when she told me that the shoes disappeared. I couldn't believe my ears. I was frustrated. I asked her, "How come you never told me this before, *poukisa*?" (Why?)

Grandma replied, "I didn't want to see the reaction that I'm seeing right now."

"But grandma what happened? When did this happen? *Pale avek mwen!* (Talk to me!)" I said angrily.

She responded, "Calm down honey, one question at a time." Tears started coming down her eyes. Her crying was contagious. I wanted to cry, too, but I couldn't because my anger was stronger than my tears.

I never truly knew why Grandpa Fanis gave me the yellow wooden shoes. After what I had to go through, I realized that a gift is not about its physical appearance, but about how meaningful it is to you. Although the shoes aren't physically with me, they are mentally a part of me. The shoes are meaningful to me because, first, they were a gift from the most admirable man in my life. Secondly, the shoes were the tools that Grandpa Fanis used to keep his family from falling apart. They remind me of how many sacrifices, struggles, and efforts he made to provide for his family in a country where you have to be thankful and appreciate everything given to you. When a gift is so important, such as the shoes are to me, the only way that I can express myself is by writing about it.[4]

4   Cassania Gilson, "Wooden Shoes," in *I Want You to Have This: A Collection of Objects and Their Stories from Around the World,* written by eleventh graders from Boston International High School (Boston, MA: 826 Boston, 2013), 94–97.

Black Belt

Marc, an 18-year-old student in Boston who emigrated from Haiti, wrote about the karate black belt his older brother gave him and how it represents an important legacy.

I wasn't ready to take the world on my own. When I heard the terrible news about my beloved brother, I was caught off guard. My guardian had passed away. After my father abandoned us, my brother was like a father to me. He had been there for me, supported me, and stuck with me through stick and stone. No matter what, he never failed to protect me. I was a hotheaded young kid. I couldn't control my emotions. All I used to do was smash things and bounce around like a pinball: bong, ping, ding. But I always lost the game. My brother, with his kindness, spoke to me and gave me advice, calmed me down, and taught me to have a bit of self-control. I didn't know the way of life until my brother took me under his wings and showed me the path to travel on.

He had been my idol way before I knew the karate star that he was. He answered to Jackson, but went by Jacky on the street. He inherited the name for being a fanatic of Jackie Chan's movies. My brother had been learning self-defense since he was twelve years old. He was a courageous and highly passionate athlete. He was such an expert at Taekwondo that he developed a habit—in other words, he was addicted. He was dedicated, never hesitated to act on his quick reflex, and never backed down from any fight. Because of his kindness, as soon as my brother went into the martial arts club, everybody had to stand by to salute him as a leader. After the formal greeting of respect, the informal greetings began. Members of the club exchanged the secret handshake with him, and others slapped hands with him. In my mind, I can still see how happy he was, with a smile on his face, talking with his friends. Everyone wanted to have a conversation with him. He was determined to lead the club as a good Samaritan, which means to have to be a community leader. He did that really well.

From my perspective, my brother was a giant because Jacky was not only a hero, he was also a counselor for me. He used to try to convince me to follow in his footsteps, to become an athlete like him. One day he took me to Julian Martial Arts with him, and the way I saw the others practicing karate seemed like military training. I was having a bad feeling, as if I did not belong in that place. Jacky could read my feelings by looking at my face, so he took me to an empty room and had a small talk with me.

He said, "What's the matter?"

"I don't think it's a great idea to follow your footsteps because I'm not the type of person that you are," I replied. "Doing karate is not in my nature."

He held my hand and told me, "Listen brother, don't ever believe or listen to people who say you can't do anything. Rapidly throw those stupid ideas out and do your thing. Otherwise, you will never succeed in life. You have to see yourself as a genius."

Then one day, Jacky gave me something more than advice. "I am going to a competition sponsored by the mayor," he told me. "I want you to have this." He handed me his black karate belt.

Ever since I found out about the tragic news a few months later, that my beloved brother had died, I have had to take care of myself and my family. Keeping Jacky's black karate belt close to my heart, I have tried to follow in his footsteps. No matter how hard, I have to do what it takes to show him that his advice to me was not in vain.[5]

---

5 Marc Scutt, "Black Belt," in *I Want You to Have This: A Collection of Objects and Their Stories from Around the World,* written by eleventh graders from Boston International High School (Boston, MA: 826 Boston, 2013), 22.

A Strength of My Neighborhood

Juan, a high school student in California, came to the United States when he was three, and he was raised in New York and Los Angeles. He writes about his neighborhood in Los Angeles and how it helps him feel connected to the culture and traditions of his family's "old world" heritage in Mexico.

One of the strengths of my neighborhood is that we gather to celebrate a special day in honor of our lady, the Virgin Guadalupe. The Virgin of Guadalupe is the mother of Jesus Christ, and she is celebrated in the Mexican community because she has appeared in many locations throughout Mexico. On the Day of Our Lady of Guadalupe, friends and families walk on the streets with votives showing her image. We also sing church music, and sometimes it feels like we're on American Idol because people are all competing against each other to see who can sing the loudest. The men dress in slacks and nice shirts, and the women look beautiful in their best dresses and high-heeled shoes. The air smells of cookies and fruit punch spiked with tequila.

Once we finish walking the neighborhood, all the children and adults have drinks in their hands. One of my favorites is called champurado. Champurado is a special drink made by many Mexican families, similar to hot chocolate. My grandmother Lucy makes it, as well as her sweet tamales flavored with pineapples, strawberry, and apple. The pineapple, or piña, tamal is a special recipe passed down in her family through the generations. The recipe came from Sinaloa (the state in Mexico where I was born). It has a juicy, delicious pineapple taste. I always get a stomach ache from eating too many of my grandmother Lucy's tamales.

When I was thirteen, I got to spend some time with my loving grandparents on their farm in Mexico. They live far from Los Angeles, on a ranch in a small, beautiful pueblo in San Ignacio. It's peaceful for them to live there because there isn't much noise like in the city. When I went to visit them, I felt excited because there were so many farm animals, like horses, sheep, chickens, and the fattest pigs you would ever find in the world (because they ate too much corn). It was on their farm I got to ride my first horse. I was petrified because I thought the horse would get furious and drop me, which it did. But once I learned how to ride a horse better, I went off riding to the river, alone, like an adult. The river was only a few minutes away from the ranch, and the view from there was really beautiful, especially when it rained.

We bring the traditions of Mexico to LA because they help us feel at home and remember the way things were before we left for more jobs and a better life in the States—traditions like the Virgin of Guadalupe celebration, family recipes, banda music and sports like ulama. I am reminded of the old world through these traditions. Even the ones we no longer celebrate create memories of my home here in Boyle Heights and my home far away from Los Angeles.[6]

6 Juan Chavez, "A Strength of My Neighborhood," in *We Are Alive When We Speak for Justice* (Los Angeles, CA: 826 Los Angeles, 2015), 185–186.

Family Names

Ralph Ellison wrote, "It is through our names that we first place ourselves in the world. Our names, being the gift of others, must be made our own. . . . They must become our masks and our shields and the containers of all those values and traditions which we learn and/or imagine as being the meaning of our familial past."[7] In the documentary *Family Name,* filmmaker Macky Alston, who is white, uncovers the history that unites three present-day families that share his last name—two black and one white. Alston introduces himself in the film with these words:

> My grandfather's name was Wallace McPherson Alston and he was a preacher. My father's name is Wallace McPherson Alston, Jr., and he's also a preacher. My name is Wallace McPherson Alston the third. I dropped out of seminary after two years. Okay, so I rebelled. . . . When I was five [my father] put me in a predominately black public school in Durham, North Carolina. It was where I first met black children with the same last name as me. I remember wondering how this could be, but I felt like this was something I couldn't talk about. We moved north when I was eight and the issue never really came up again.
>
> Recently I asked my dad about our family history and he gave me a book. That's where I discovered that the Alstons were one of the largest slave-owning families in North Carolina.
>
> Is something a secret if everybody knows it, but nobody talks about it? I want to know the whole story behind my family name.[8]

For many of us, our names can help us learn about our family histories and, ultimately, about ourselves.Names not only represent our identities but also reflect our relationship to society. Throughout history, names have represented, in a variety of ways, one's degree of power and freedom. In the book *Parting the Waters,* historian Taylor Branch writes, "Among the most joyous feelings most frequently mentioned by freed or escaped slaves was the freedom to choose a name. A name was no longer incidental."[9]

7   Ralph Ellison, in *The Collected Essays of Ralph Ellison,* ed. John F. Callahan (Modern Library, 2003), 192.
8   *Family Name,* directed by Macky Alston (Opelika Pictures, 1997).
9   Taylor Branch, *Parting the Waters: America in the King Years, 1954–63* (New York: Simon & Schuster, 1988), 45.

LESSON 6

Many Voices, One National Identity

Materials

VIDEO:
American ID: Three Words

READING:
Shifting Demographics in the United States

READING:
What Does It Mean to "Be American"?

TEACHING STRATEGY:
Identity Charts

TEACHING STRATEGY:
Save the Last Word for Me

Find the materials you will need to teach this lesson plan at **hstry.is/mypart**.

Essential Questions

- **Where does a nation's identity come from? How can individuals with so many different identities come together to form a national identity?**
- **What is the national identity of the United States, and how does it relate to each of us as individuals?**

Overview

The goal of this final lesson is to provide a bridge from the examination of individual identity in prior lessons to the study of the history, literature, or civics of the United States with which students will engage throughout the rest of the year.

Students will start the lesson by considering the idea that nations, like individuals, have identities. They will also consider the relationship between a nation's identity and the identities of the individuals who comprise that nation. Then they will look at evidence of the changing demographics and increasing diversity of the United States and analyze what that information suggests about the complexity of the country's national identity. Finally, students will respond to the idea that a cohesive national identity requires knowledge and values shared by all individuals in a nation, and they will consider a variety of ideas about the knowledge and values that unite Americans.

In this lesson, and through the course that follows, students will discover that the identity of the United States is the product of interactions between many different groups, or communities, and many different types of people. Thus, the choices people make about their identities, and the way they live with others, all contribute to the national narrative as well as to the national identity. Students will also discover that, because people with so many different backgrounds have contributed to the identity of the United States, the ways that people think about the United States often vary and sometimes conflict with one another. That tension itself might be part of how one defines American identity.

As students continue to study American history, literature, or civics, they will hopefully be able to recognize some of these themes of identity: the choices, the labels, and the legacies that inform what the United States of America has been and continues to become. More important is the hope that they will be able to recognize their part in the narrative of the United States and their ability to influence the next part of the story.

Activities

1. Begin an Identity Chart for the United States

This activity introduces students to the concept of national identity. Students then draw upon their initial thoughts about American identity from the beginning of the unit to begin an identity chart for the United States.

- Explain to students that just like individuals have identities, so do nations. Ask students to think or write quietly about the following questions: Where does a nation's identity come from? How can individuals with so many different identities come together to form a national identity?

- Next, start an identity chart for the United States. Ideally, you can create the identity chart on a large piece of paper that can be posted in the classroom. You will return to the chart throughout this lesson.

- Ask students to recall the first lesson in this unit, when they drew pictures to illustrate an "American" and analyzed the Flag of Faces. (You might even show this image again now.) Ask students what words, phrases, or images should be added to the class identity chart for the United States based on this initial thinking.

- Then ask students to brainstorm in their journals any other words or phrases that come to mind that they think describe the identity of the United States.

2. Gather Additional Evidence about the Identity of the United States

Students will watch a short video and use a report on the changing demographics of the United States to identify additional words and phrases to add to their identity chart for the United States.

- Show students the video American ID: Three Words at hstry.is/mypart. Ask students to write down three to five words used in the video to describe American identity. Then lead a class discussion about the video, using the following questions:
  - What common themes did you notice in the video related to how people around the world view American identity?
  - Where do you think people's ideas about American identity come from?
  - What are some of the labels people use to describe the United States? What are some of the assumptions they make?
  - Which labels and assumptions from the video ring true, based on your own experience? Which feel untrue to you?
  - Which words and phrases from the video should we add to our identity chart for the United States?

- Share with students the reading Shifting Demographics in the United States. The data in this reading will help to illustrate the complicated relationship between individual and national identity in the United States. Read it together as a class, and clarify language and statistics for students as necessary.

- Divide the class into pairs or small groups, and assign one paragraph of Shifting Demographics in the United States to each group. It will be each group's task to dig into their assigned paragraph, discuss its meaning, and use it to come up with another item to add to the identity chart for the United States. Each group's item might be a statistic or direct quotation from their paragraph, or they might come up with their own word or phrase that summarizes their understanding of the paragraph.

- After groups have completed their tasks, ask a member from each group to add their group's item to the class identity chart.

- At this point in the lesson, lead the class in a short discussion to take stock of the characteristics on the identity chart. What conclusions can they draw so far about the national identity of the United States? What questions do they have?

3. Explore Common Knowledge and Values among Americans

In this activity, students will be introduced to the idea that a national identity is more than a list of diverse qualities and characteristics of the citizenry; it is also a collection of knowledge and values shared across the nation. This idea sets up a tension between the identities of individuals and the collective identity of a nation.

- Now that students have begun the process of characterizing a national identity for the United States, share with them the following quotation from author and educator Eric Liu:

    The . . . challenge, for Americans new and old, is to make a common culture that's greater than the sum of our increasingly diverse parts. It's not enough for the United States to be a neutral zone where a million little niches of identity might flourish; in order to make our diversity a true asset, we need those niches to be able to share a vocabulary. We need to be able to have a broad base of common knowledge so that our diversity can be most fully activated.[1]

- Have students work with a partner to answer the following questions:

    - What is Eric Liu saying about national identity in the United States? Explain this quotation in your own words.

    - Do you agree with Liu? Why or why not?

- Pass out the reading What Does It Mean to "Be American"? The reading includes quotations from a variety of people saying what they think are examples of the common knowledge and values that unite individual Americans in the identity of the United States.

- Students will individually read through the quotations and choose one that they have a strong reaction to. They should copy the quotation into their journals. (If it is especially long, they might simply copy the first sentence.) Then they will respond to the quotation. Do they agree with it? Is it consistent with

1 Eric Liu, "What Every American Should Know," *The Atlantic,* July 3, 2015, https://www.theatlantic.com/politics/archive/2015/07/what-every-american-should-know/397334/.

their experience of the United States? Or do they think it is incorrect or misguided? Why?

- Students will then share and discuss the quotations they chose and responded to in small groups, using the Save the Last Word for Me strategy.

- Once the small group discussions are complete, bring the whole group together to debrief the activity with the following questions:

  - What characteristics do you want to add to the identity chart for the United States? Are there any you want to remove?

  - How has your thinking about the national identity of the United States evolved?

  - What did you learn from each other in your discussions? What ideas from your discussions especially resonated with you?

- If possible, keep the identity chart visible in the classroom throughout the year. The class can return to it and discuss ways they might revise it based on what they learn about the United States throughout the course.

Shifting Demographics in the United States

Just as it has changed throughout history, the identity of the United States continues to evolve. The next chapter of the American narrative is being written by an increasingly diverse population. The excerpts below, taken from a Pew Research Center article on top demographic trends currently shaping the United States and the world, explore some of the population shifts that will affect this narrative.

Americans are more racially and ethnically diverse than in the past, and the U.S. is projected to be even more diverse in the coming decades. By 2055, the U.S. will not have a single racial or ethnic majority. Much of this change has been (and will be) driven by immigration. Nearly 59 million immigrants have arrived in the U.S. in the past 50 years, mostly from Latin America and Asia. Today, a near-record 14% of the country's population is foreign born compared with just 5% in 1965. Over the next five decades, the majority of U.S. population growth is projected to be linked to new Asian and Hispanic immigration . . .

Asia has replaced Latin America (including Mexico) as the biggest source of new immigrants to the U.S. In a reversal of one of the largest mass migrations in modern history, net migration flows from Mexico to the U.S. turned negative between 2009 and 2014, as more Mexicans went home than arrived in the U.S. . . . Meanwhile, Asians are now the only major racial or ethnic group whose numbers are rising mainly because of immigration. And while African immigrants make up a small share of the U.S. immigrant population, their numbers are also growing steadily—roughly doubling every decade since 1970.

America's demographic changes are shifting the electorate—and American politics. The 2016 electorate [was] the most diverse in U.S. history due to strong growth among Hispanic eligible voters, particularly U.S.-born youth. There are also wide gaps opening up between the generations on many social and political issues. Young adult

Millennials are much more likely than their elders to hold liberal views on many political and social issues, though they are also less likely to identify with either political party: 50% call themselves political independents.

Millennials, young adults born after 1980, are the new generation to watch. They have likely surpassed Baby Boomers (born 1946–1964) as the largest U.S. generation and differ significantly from their elders in many ways. They are the most racially diverse generation in American history: 43% of Millennial adults are non-white, the highest share of any generation. And while they are on track to be the most educated generation to date, this achievement has come at a cost: Many Millennials are struggling with student debt. In addition to the weak labor market of recent years, student debt is perhaps one reason why many are still living at home. Despite these troubles, Millennials are the most upbeat about their financial future: More than eight-in-ten say they either currently have enough money to lead the lives they want or expect to in the future.

Women's role in the labor force and leadership positions has grown dramatically. The labor force participation rate for American women has risen steadily since the 1960s. In fact, mothers were the sole or primary breadwinner in a record 40% of all households with children in 2011. The gender pay gap has narrowed over this period of time, especially for young women just entering the labor force, but it still persists. As more women have entered the workforce, the share of women in top leadership jobs has risen, but they still make up a small share of the nation's political and business leaders relative to men. . . .

The American family is changing. After decades of declining marriage rates, the share of American adults who have never been married is at an historic high. Two-parent households are on the decline in the U.S., while divorce, remarriage and cohabitation are on the rise. About one-in-six American kids now live in a blended family. And the roles of mothers and fathers are converging, due in part to the rise of breadwinner moms. Dads are doing more housework and child care, while moms are doing more paid work outside the home. . . .

The share of Americans who live in middle class households is shrinking. The share of U.S. adults living in middle-income households fell to 50% in 2015, after more than four decades in which those households served as the nation's economic majority. And the financial gaps between middle- and upper-income Americans have widened, with upper-income households holding 49% of U.S. aggregate household income (up from 29% in 1970) and seven times as much wealth as middle-income households (up from three times as much in 1983). . . .

Christians are declining as a share of the U.S. population, and the number of U.S. adults who do not identify with any organized religion has grown. While the U.S. remains home to more Christians than any other country, the percentage of Americans identifying as Christian dropped from 78% in 2007 to 71% in 2014. By contrast, the religiously unaffiliated have surged seven percentage points in that time span to make up 23% of U.S. adults last year. This trend has been driven in large part by Millennials, 35% of whom are religious "nones." The rise of the "nones" is not a story unique to the U.S.: The unaffiliated are now the second-largest religious group in 48% of the world's nations. . . . [2]

2 D'Vera Cohn and Andrea Caumont, "10 demographic trends that are shaping the U.S. and the world," Pew Research Center, *Fact Tank: News in the Numbers* (blog), March 31, 2016, http://www.pewresearch.org/fact-tank/2016/03/31/10-demographic-trends-that-are-shaping-the-u-s-and-the-world/.

What Does It Mean to "Be American"?

In 2014, *New York Times* reporter Damien Cave traveled the length of highway I-35, which runs south to north through the middle of the United States, for his "The Way North" project. Along the way, he asked 35 people, "What does it mean to be American?" These are some of their answers.[3]

Becoming American means following the rules. It means respecting your neighbors, in your own neighborhood.

—Francine Sharp, 73, retired teacher in Kansas (born in Kansas)

If you work hard, you get good things in life.

—José, college student/roofer; immigrant without legal status in Tulsa, Oklahoma (born in Mexico)

Being American is making a change, and making good changes. Being American is being welcoming, being caring about other people, being proud of the country. And it's forgiveness. It's not holding grudges on anything—I mean, where's that going to get you?

—Natalie Villafranca, 14, in Texas (born in Dallas)

Being American means protection by the law. Anyone can say whatever they want and, even if I don't agree with them, they're still protected by the law it's my job to enforce. That's their freedom. That's their right.

—Sean Larkin, 40, sergeant with Tulsa Police Department's gang unit in Tulsa, Oklahoma (born in Virginia)

Being American is red, white and blue and being free. It doesn't matter what language you speak; if you're born in America, you're still American. No matter what you look like, no matter what.

—Sebastien de la Cruz, 12, student who gained attention, and backlash, when he sang the national anthem during the 2013 NBA finals in a mariachi outfit (born and lives in San Antonio)

3 All quotes except the last one (by Taylor R.) are from "Day 39: On Being American" (The Way North), *New York Times*, May 17, 2014, https://www.nytimes.com/interactive/2014/us/the-way-north.html?_r=0#p/39.

I want all girls, especially girls of color, to know that they can be a part of science. And more than that, they can be leaders in science. I want them to know that, because I know that I am America. That I am science. I'm just the part that people refuse to recognize.[4]

—Taylor R., 13, speaking about her ambitions at the March for Science in April 2017

The following excerpts are from other Americans discussing what they think it means to "be American." Among these voices are historians and writers who think about this topic a lot, as well as individuals from other walks of life who participated in a discussion for the documentary film *A More Perfect Union*.[5]

Precisely because we are not a people held together by blood, no one knows who an American is except by what they believe. It's important that we do know our history, because our history is the source of our Americanness.

—Historian Gordon Wood

When people wrote "All men are created equal," they really meant men; but they didn't mean any other men except white men who owned land. That's what they meant. But because the ideas are powerful, there's no way that they could get away with holding to that. It's not possible when you have an idea that's as powerful and as revolutionary as a country founded on the idea that just because you're in the world, just because you're here, you have a right to certain things that are common to all humanity. That's really what we say in those documents. The idea that we begin the Constitution with, "We, the People" . . . even though they didn't mean me! They had no idea I'd ever want to make a claim on that. And they'd have been horrified if they'd known that any of us would. But you can't let that powerful an idea out into the world without consequences.

—Writer Rosemary Bray

The American Dream has no meaning for me. What it was founded on, the Constitution and the Bill of Rights, in many ways I feel are used as billy clubs against minorities and cultural minorities, whether they be gay, or different in any way from the norm in this country. I, for example, don't think I'd like to go to California because of what I look like. I could be pulled over and carded, and I would have to prove my ancestry. And look how long my family has been in northern New Mexico. Ten to twelve generations!

—Vicente Martinez

4 "13-Year-Old Aspiring Astronaut's Inspirational Speech at the March for Science," *Women You Should Know* website, April 24, 2017, http://www.womenyoushouldknow.net/13-year-old-aspiring-astronauts-inspirational-speech-at-the-march-for-science/.
5 All quotes are from the online companion materials to the documentary *A More Perfect Union* (Arcadia Pictures, 1997), available at http://www.pbs.org/ampu/quotes3.html.

Unit Assessment

Consider the following ideas for a final assessment or project for this unit before launching the next part of your course on United States history, literature, or civics:

- **Interviews about American Identity:** One way to continue students' inquiry into the connections between individual identity and the identity of the United States is to have them interview others in the school or community to find additional perspectives in response to the question, "What does it mean to 'be American'?" As a minimum, they should interview three other students and three adults. Students could record others' responses to this question and create a short video (with their phones), or they might transcribe the answers. Either way, they should accompany their findings with a paragraph discussing the common themes that they heard, as well as the ways their own research either connects to or differs from the ideas they encountered in this lesson.

- **Inquiry Questions:** Another way to assess students' thinking about the identity of the United States and to help pivot toward the country's history or literature is to enlist the class in creating a list of inquiry questions for the year. In this last lesson, students' thinking has been made visible in a variety of ways, including the identity chart the class created for the United States. They might now pause and ask, for example: Why do some people think being American is about arrogance, while others think it is about generosity? Or: What is it about the history of the United States that leads to different ideas about what American identity really is? At the end of class or for homework, ask each student to survey all of the ideas that they and their classmates have written down and write two questions that they would like to find answers to over the course of their study of the United States. As you read and evaluate students' questions, you might group and synthesize them (to eliminate repetition) and compile a shorter list of questions that you can post in the classroom and return to throughout the year.

Credits

Grateful acknowledgment is made for permission to reproduce the following:

Foreword from *We Turned Back to See Where We Came from: Snapshots, Vignettes, and Stories* by Maria Hinojosa. Reproduced by permission of 826 Boston, 826boston.org.

"Still Me Inside" by Mai Goda, from *Chicken Soup for the Teen Soul*, by Jack Canfield, Mark Victor Hansen, Stephanie H. Meyer, and John Meyer. Copyright
© 2012 by Chicken Soup for the Soul Publishing, LLC. Reproduced by permission. All rights reserved.

"Computer Keyboard" by Gerard Kasemba, "The Wooden Shoes" by Cassania Gilson, and "Black Belt" by Marc Scutt, all taken from *I Want You to Have This: A Collection of Objects and Their Stories from Around the World*. Reproduced by permission of 826 Boston, 826boston.org.

"Chameleon" by David Lopera, taken from *It's Not the Stone that Brings You Strength.* Reproduced by permission of 826 Boston, 826boston.org.

Excerpted version of "What Are You?" by Anna Fitzpatrick, in *Rookie Magazine*, June 13, 2013, www.rookiemag.com. Reproduced by permission of Anna Fitzpatrick.

"A Strength of My Neighborhood" by Juan Chavez, taken from *We Are Alive When We Speak for Justice.* Reproduced by permission of 826 Boston, 826boston.org.

From *Questions for Ada* by Ijeoma Umebinyuo. Copyright © 2016 by Ijeoma Umebinyuo. Reproduced by permission of Ijeoma Umebinyuo.

www.ingramcontent.com/pod-product-compliance
Lightning Source LLC
Chambersburg PA
CBHW041430270326
41933CB00027B/3499